THE MOSAICS OF
PIAZZA ARMERINA

THE ROMAN VILLA AT CASALE AND MORGANTINA
3rd-4th centuries A.D.

Editions KINA ITALIA

© **KINA Italia S.p.A.** - Milan
Texts: Claudia Converso
Translations: A.B.A. - Milan
Photo: Francesco Paolo Scalea
Graphics and printing: KINA Italia S.p.A. - Milan
All rights in texts and photographs reserved.
Reproduction prohibited.
Our thanks to Lucia Calabrese for her technical assistance.

DISTRIBUTION
Edizioni Amoroso Vincenzo Srl
Cartoleria Ingrosso
Via F. Purpura, 25/27
Tel. (091) 6162945 - Fax 6164270
90127 PALERMO

INTRODUCTION

Piazza Armerina, the Roman villa at Casale and Morgantina are set amid the lush countryside of Enna Province; each one of the three holds its own important place in the history of Sicily and Italy, and together they form a triangle of great archaeological, artistic and cultural importance.

The Roman villa at Casale was built as a hunting lodge for Maximian Herculius and his family between the 3rd and 4th centuries A.D. Maximian shared with Valerius Diocletian the title of Emperor Augustus of the Roman Empire (which he received in 286 A.D.), with command over the Western part of the Empire. The special form of government under which they ruled was the Tetrarchy, which comprised two Emperors and two Caesars who were supposed to succeed them after 20 years (Galerius was Diocletian's Caesar, and Constantius Chlorus, succeeded on his death by his son Constantine, was Maximian's). Maximian was forced first to abdicate and then to flee to Gaul in the difficult period of Constantine's rise to power, and committed suicide in 310 A.D. after being accused of treason.

The construction of the villa, which partly stands on the site of an earlier building, presumably began after 293 A.D.; Maximian very probably established his residence there some 10 years later, after his abdication. The luxurious mansion continued to be used after Maximian's death, as demonstrated by traces of successive rebuilding work on the structure dating from the 6th-7th centuries. When the Arabs invaded Sicily the villa was abandoned, but around the year 1000 it was inhabited again for a period, this time by the Normans, who made further modifications that are still visible in its layout today. The decline of the magnificent building began when fire broke out during the revolt of the Lombard militia against William the Bad.

The itinerary described in this book opens with a visit to the Roman Villa at Casale, in homage to one of the most magnificent and significant examples of Roman art in Italy. The villa, astonishing for its size and the elegance of its architecture, contains some mosaic floors of exceptional beauty and figurative vivacity, exemplified by the famous mosaic in the Great Hunt ambulatory, which are protected by an ingenious roof that for once combines modern construction criteria with preservation of the original forms. This is followed by a visit to Piazza Armerina, unfairly famed only for its closeness to the Imperial residence, whereas it contains a wealth of artistic and architectural treasures, mainly from the Mediaeval and Baroque periods, scattered over an urban area on which history has left indelible traces. The itinerary concludes with a description of the excavations at Morgantina, a gem of Graeco-Roman archaeology which holds more than one monument worthy of the visitor's interest.

THE ROMAN VILLA AT CASALE

The Roman Villa at Casale, custodian of some of the most precious artistic treasures of the Roman age to have survived to the present day, stands at the foot of Mount Mangone near Piazza Armerina. After some chance finds during the 18th century, excavations began in the first 20 years of the 19th, but it was not until the end of the 19th century that excavation work began in earnest, proceeding with more modern, scientific criteria until the mid-20th century and then to the present day. The excavation work has brought to light the majestic palace of a residential complex which covered an area of over 3500 sq.m. and comprised numerous rooms decorated with splendid mosaic floors of the African school, nearly all of which are in an excellent state of preservation. The terraced plan of the villa, which was built as a hunting lodge for the Emperor Maximian Herculius between the 3rd and 4th centuries A.D. on the site of a much smaller existing building, follows the lie of the gently sloping land on which it stands. There are four main groups of rooms, connected by staircases, tunnels and corridors: the atrium and baths area, the peristyle and living rooms, the triclinium and xystus, the private rooms and the great basilica.

1) Ancient Roman coins
2) Entrance to the villa
3) View of large peristyle

THE ENTRANCE AND THE POLYGONAL COURTYARD

If you follow the drive leading to the villa, flanked on the left by the ruins of the high wall of the aqueduct that supplied the swimming pool and the baths area of the villa overlooking it, you will soon reach the monumental entrance where the road that joined the public highway leading to Catania and Agrigento began.

Three arched doorways (the largest one, in the centre, is 4.5 m wide, while the smaller ones on either side are just over 2.50 m wide), originally flanked by stout marble columns, led to the interior of the villa.

The characteristic feature of the entrance is the two large nymphaeum-niches, fitted with basins originally covered inside and out with white mosaic, some of which still remains. The function of these large niches must have been not only decorative, but also to collect the water stored in the attic over the entrance, evidently used as a storage tank. The entrance gives onto the atrium, formed at the centre of a magnificent polygonal courtyard around which an elegant porticoed corridor runs.

In the middle of the courtyard, where the remains of the original white stone paving can be seen, is the bed of a square fountain in which rainwater was collected and then directed through an underground channel to the large latrine nearby. The marble columns with Ionic capitals for-

1

ming the portico, ornamented in some sections by the remains of multicoloured mosaic floor decoration, are interrupted along the right-hand side to make room for the staircase that leads to the large peristyle on the upper terrace. At the end of the portico there is a small square aedicule with an apse, its floor decorated by elegant mosaics, which gave onto the large latrine and the palaestra. On the right-hand side of the aedicule is a vestibule leading to the palaestra and the baths, with frescoed walls and an attractive mosaic floor with geometrical patterns.

1) View of entrance and polygonal courtyard
2) Coat-of-arms of the Tetrarchy:
*   fresco technique*

THE PRAEFURNIA

Along the western side of the calidaria there are three furnaces (praefurnia), two lateral and one central, designed to heat the air and water used in the baths. The central furnace had a large basin containing water which was heated to the right temperature and then conveyed to the calidarium pools through special lead pipes (fistulae). The walls of the furnaces reveal the presence of brick pipes (tubuli), which served an insulation purpose here. The air heated by the furnaces was conveyed into the cavity of the hypocaustum, and from there to the calidaria.

THE CALIDARIA

The three calidarium rooms, used for hot baths and saunas, were situated along the west side of the tepidarium, to which they were connected by two openings. The rooms on either side contained bathing pools, one rectangular (probably reserved for men) and one semicircular (perhaps used by women), while the central section was the laconicum (sauna room). As the original mosaic-covered floors of all three rooms are missing, the structure of the hypocaustum below, which allowed upward circulation of warm air through special brick pipes in the walls, can clearly be seen.

Baths: the praefurnia

THE TEPIDARIUM

This room, situated between the calidaria and the frigidarium, enabled the body temperature to be reduced gradually by taking a lukewarm bath after the hot bath and before the cold bath, which was followed by a massage and cleansing of sweat in the unctiones room. The tepidarium, which has an elongated shape with two apses closing the shorter sides, imitates the layout of the palaestra. The room must originally have been roofed with cross-vaults; little remains of the floor, although a covering mosaic depicting a circus subject can still be identified. It probably portrayed the ludi cursori (running races), and especially scenes from a lampadedromia, a kind of race in which the competitors (men or women) held a flaming torch, as demonstrated by the naked busts of men shown running with a torch in their right hand and a shield in the left. The absence of much of the floor reveals the supporting structure (hypocaustum), which consists of small brick pilasters resting on a foundation; its purpose was to circulate the warm air attracted by the praefurnia of the calidaria, allowing it to rise through special pipes to the tepidarium.

General view of tepidarium

THE ANOINTING ROOM

This small square room, which connected the frigidarium to the tepidarium, was probably used for unctiones (massage, anointing and cleansing after bathing). The floor mosaic in the room, some parts of which are sadly missing, supports this theory. The mosaic is framed by a simple border consisting of strips and zigzag patterns; in the middle of the upper register stands a headless male figure, naked and muscular, with a naked slave on his left, massaging his shoulder and arm, and another naked slave on his right (of whom only the right arm and the lower part of the body are still visible), holding the strigil used to scrape off sweat and a bottle of anointing oil. In the lower register two more slaves, their loins covered with a strip of cloth bearing their names (Tite on the left and Cassi on the right) are holding a bucket and a broom respectively. Both these characters have their neck and chest decorated by a collar with a pendant, and the one on the right is wearing an unusual conical hat of Syrian origin.

The floor

12

THE FRIGIDARIUM

The cold bathing room is octagonal, with six large recesses along the sides adjacent to the palaestra and the opposite sides, which gave onto the anointing room; two pools were installed along the other two opposite sides. The central area, originally roofed with a mosaic-lined dome, has a floor mosaic with a marine scene featuring mythological characters and amorini. In the recesses, four of which served as changing rooms and two as vestibules, members of the Imperial family are shown at the baths. The smaller pool, which has a trefoil plan, was used for warm baths, and the other one, which was much larger, with an elongated shape, was used for swimming.

General view of exterior and interior of frigidarium, and detail of floor mosaic

THE BATHS VESTIBULE

This square room of modest size is situated along the porticoed side of the polygonal courtyard opposite the entrance to the villa, behind the Ionic columns.

From the vestibule, the service staff could go through an arched doorway to the palaestra, and from there to the baths area. The walls of the room still retain a few traces of the original frescoes, while the floor is covered with an elegant mosaic featuring geometrical patterns surrounded by a fret with a single key pattern. Braided coloured ribbons wind through the composition in an elegant play of colour, turning into crosses, ovals and octagons framing decorative patterns of composite flowers and rosettes.

THE VENUS AEDICULE

This small square room with an apse at the end, situated on the left-hand side of the baths vestibule, owes its name to the fragments of a marble statue of the goddess Venus found there. Once again, the floor is decorated with a multicoloured mosaic in geometrical patterns. The apse is decorated with a composition (only part of which has survived) featuring diamond shapes against a latticework background. The preceding square chamber is decorated with more diamonds with an elongated flower in the middle, alternating with squares formed by lines and braids framing a rosette.

1) Palaestra
2) Baths vestibule reserved for servants
3) Detail of floor of the Venus Aedicule

THE LARGE LATRINE

This latrine, designed for those who did not have access to the villa, is situated on the left-hand side of the polygonal courtyard; from here, a small vestibule with a black and white mosaic floor led to the large exedral room fitted with marble seats with holes in the middle (now lost). The cloaca which ran under the seats was connected by a channel to the nearby River Gela, into which the sewage flowed. The central part of the latrine was open to the sky and paved with ordinary bricks, while the part fitted with seats was sheltered by a lean-to roof resting on four columns, and the floor had a mosaic decoration with black and white tesserae.

General view of the large latrine

THE ADVENTUS VESTIBULE

This large quadrangular room is situated at the end of the staircase which leads from the courtyard to the upper terrace, giving access to the main villa. The tablinum contains the well-preserved remains of the elegant mosaic floor after which it is named, portraying the ritual salute made to the Emperor by the servants and procuratores of the villa on his arrival (adventus). An elegant multicoloured frame with geometrical patterns surrounds the scene, which covers two registers; sadly, many of the characters which must originally have been portrayed are missing. The lower register depicts three young men in vividly embroidered garments, wearing wreaths made of sprigs of greenery and holding a diptych to welcome the master of the house; the upper register shows two more young men wearing wreaths and holding a laurel branch, and an older-looking man holding a bronze candelabrum with a lit candle. All the characters are looking to the right, where the figure of the Emperor must originally have been.

Detail and general view of mosaic floor portraying characters welcoming the Emperor. Small photo: the lararium

THE PERISTYLE

The Adventus Vestibule gives onto the large peristyle, also built on the upper terrace of the villa. The peristyle was preceded by a rectangular apsidal aedicule, situated opposite the vestibule, which acted as the lararium. The small room, used as a sacellum for the traditional cult of the deified dead, contained a sacrificial altar and a statue (now lost), and has a splendid hedera (ivy) mosaic on the floor. This complex multicoloured decoration features an octagon, formed by two overlapping squares with vivid braid patterns, framed by a variegated border with red and white meander patterns. In the middle of the octagon is a laurel wreath bound with a purplered ribbon surrounding a leaf of ivy, the plant sacred to the god Dionysus and to Hercules, which later became the symbol of the villa's owner, Emperor Maximian Herculius, and his family. The symbolic motif, present in many of the mosaics decorating the villa, also appears in the decorative strip at the base, with a black-leaved ivy shoot.

In this magnificent hunting lodge, the great peristyle, which represents the heart of the villa around which all the other official and private rooms are distributed, replaces the ancient atrium characteristic of the Roman villas of an earlier period. The peristyle, of clearly Hellenistic derivation, fulfilled both a decorative architectural function and the practical function of providing excellent lighting for the various rooms that gave onto it. It consists of a

Detail of peristyle

large rectangular courtyard surrounded by a colonnaded portico, now protected, like most of the building, by a modern roof specially designed by architect Minissi. In the middle of the courtyard stands the elegant irregularly-shaped basin of the fountain, decorated by a small statue of Eros. The erotes of Hellenic mythology (the cupids of Roman mythological tradition) were classically portrayed in Graeco-Roman art as chubby winged children, and usually appear in joyful, carefree or romantic scenes. It was believed that the arrows shot by their bows had the power to cause their victim (human or god) to fall in love. The inner edges of the basin were decorated with an elegant mosaic pattern of coloured fish that appeared just above the surface of the water; originally, the fountain was almost certainly surrounded by a lush garden, which contained not only flowering plants and shrubs but also tall trees providing protection from the light and shade from the sun. The marble columns of the portico (10 along the longer sides and 8 along the shorter sides), surmounted by Corinthian capitals, supported the architraves on which the lean-to roofs over the courtyard originally rested. The bases of the columns, some of which were of different heights and therefore stood on blocks of masonry, were connected by a low wall made of masonry but with a more elegant marble facing, on which stood elegant plutei depicting pairs of facing dolphins, one of which can still be seen near the small lararium at the entrance.

Side view of peristyle

The corridors of the portico feature a magnificent mosaic floor decoration of elegant, complex workmanship. Laurel wreaths of green leaves on a black background tied with a dark pink ribbon alternating with wreaths of gilded leaves against a red background tied with a green ribbon are enclosed in panels bordered by the coloured patterns formed by three interwoven coloured ribbons. Each wreath, decorated at the corners of the squares by ivy leaves and facing figures of small birds, surrounds a multicoloured figure in which the head of a wild or domestic animal is represented with surprising realism, sometimes in a front view, sometimes a three-quarter view, and sometimes in profile.

In the eastern part of the portico, where the staircase is situated, these animal subjects are replaced by a mosaic floor which is also multicoloured but features geometrical patterns surrounded by braids of coloured ribbon. At the point where the mosaic portraying animals' heads is interrupted to make way for this decoration, two white strips appear on the right and left, both decorated in the centre by a picture of a gilded vase with two red handles, from which branches of green ivy trail off on either side. The decorative strip facing west, on which the name Bonufatius can be read, dates from a renovation carried out during the Byzantine period.

Recent studies have established that the portico comprised two separate routes, a private one to the left and one used for official events and meetings on the right, both of which led to the Great Hunt courtyard which stands in front of the lararium, at the entrance to the peristyle. Along the side on which the ambulatory

is situated there are three staircases, each consisting of seven steps; the central staircase led from the Great Hunt corridor to the peristyle, while the two lateral staircases were used in the opposite direction, to gain access from the portico to the ambulatory.

As already mentioned, the various rooms of the villa are built around the peristyle; some of them open directly onto the portico, which was reached via staircases, entrances and corridors interconnected in such a way that practically any part of the villa could be reached from this central point.

General view and details of medallioned floor portraying heads of animals

THE SMALL LATRINE

This small room was connected to the peristyle by a door that led to a trapezoidal open air courtyard paved with simple square brick tiles. The courtyard, which was designed to aerate the nearby room, gives onto the latrine itself, also trapezoidal, with the longer side curved.

Seats with holes in the middle, under which the cloaca ran, were installed along the curved and straight sides.

The floor (which had a small marble-lined tank in one corner to supply water to the cloaca) is decorated with a mosaic on a white background portraying a partridge, a great bustard, an ocelot, a hare and a wild ass. The walls were originally covered with plaster with a fake marble finish.

The small latrine

Page 27: Views of floor portraying episodes from four-horse chariot races

THE PALAESTRA

This large room, terminating in two apses on the shorter sides, contained the villa's palaestra, which was accessed from the baths area. The floor is entirely covered by a magnificent, complex mosaic portraying scenes from the chariot races held at the Circus Maximus in Rome. Four factions took part, each of which was distinguished by a different colour (green, red, blue or white) and represented by two four-horse chariots. The chariots entered the arena through the gates of the carceres and entertained the public with a daredevil race (the mosaic shows a collision between two chariots); they drove round the central spina, which was bounded at the ends by the metae with three conical columns, and decorated with the obelisk of Augustus. The three temples consecrated to Rome, Jupiter and Hercules can be seen in the north apse.

THE TRAPEZOIDAL VESTIBULE

This room, which has a trapezoid plan as its name indicates, is situated almost at the corner between the north and west sides of the peristyle, and connects the upper terrace of the villa to the lower baths area. This was certainly the vestibule used by the Imperial family and guests to reach the palaestra, which gave access to the baths, while the servants and staff reached the baths area through the vestibule leading off the porticoed courtyard on the lower level of the villa. A bench with fragments of the original white stone facing runs along the walls of the room. The exquisite mosaic floor is dominated by a family scene in which Eutropia, wife of the Emperor Maximian and consequently domina of the villa, takes her children Maxentius and Fausta to the baths. An aspect worthy of note, apart from Eutropia's hairstyle, which was characteristic of the period, is the realism with which the artists portrayed Maxentius' squint, by using one square and one triangular tessera for his pupils. Next to Fausta and Maxentius are two serving girls; the first is carrying a basket, which presumably contains clean clothes, while the second holds a box containing oil and balsams for the unctiones.

Eutropia, the "domina of the villa"

THE KILN ROOM

The first of the rooms situated along the north side of the peristyle is called the Kiln Room because a kiln for firing vases was installed on the right-hand side during the Norman period. The floor is decorated with an elegant multicoloured mosaic with geometrical patterns featuring hexagons, crosses and octagons.

Detail of floor

INTERMEDIATE ROOM

This rectangular room which, like the one preceding it, was used by the servants who looked after the villa's guests, has a plain floor mosaic dominated by black and white geometrical patterns with squares, hexagons and five-pointed stars which contain other decorative patterns in pale shades.

Floor detail

KITCHEN

The floor of the rectangular kitchen was decorated with a figured mosaic of which no trace remains, as it was replaced with stone slabs during the late Imperial period.

The large basin covered with white tesserae was installed during the Norman period. This kitchen was used to prepare food for guests.

Kitchen

THE DANCE ROOM

This large rectangular chamber adjacent to the kiln room contains the remains of wall frescoes and a partly damaged mosaic floor with scenes divided into two registers, depicting dancing couples with youths lifting two girls, and a girl dressed in a tunic, lifting her veil as she dances.

Detail of floor

THE STAR MOSAIC ROOM

The floor has an elegant, though partly damaged mosaic with multi-coloured geometrical patterns. Eight-pointed stars, formed by two superimposed squares with a double-braid border, enclose octagons decorated with rosettes or woven ribbons framed by a ring of elegant diamonds.

General view of floor mosaic

THE LOST MOSAIC ROOM

The Star Mosaic Room gives onto this rectangular chamber, the floor of which was originally decorated with a figured mosaic. In the Norman period the use of the room changed, and the mosaic was replaced with simple stone slabs.

Lost mosaic room

THE FOUR SEASONS ROOM

This room gives onto the left-hand side of the peristyle. It is adorned with a splendid mosaic floor depicting the four seasons in tondi, each surrounded by a six-pointed star, in a magnificent play of colour and geometrical patterns. Spring is represented by a girl wearing a garland of roses on her head, summer by a young man crowned with a garland of golden ears of corn, and autumn by the gentle features of a young girl, her head reclining in melancholy; finally, winter is portrayed as a young man, his head crowned with leaves and a cloak on his left shoulder. Other tondi, alongside those of the seasons, portray birds and fish.

THE FISHING EROTES ROOM

The inner room, which leads off the previous room, was used as a triclinium for guests. Slight traces of the original frescoes remain on the walls, while the floor is decorated by a mosaic portraying four boats with erotes fishing in a sea teeming with fish. The shore and a seaside villa can be seen in the background.

1) Four Seasons Room: autumn
2) Fishing Erotes Room: detail

THE SMALL HUNT ROOM

The floor mosaic decorating this room portrays scenes from an autumn hunting party in five registers, starting with the preparations. Each episode is shown in a particular natural setting (hills, thickets and mountains can be seen) that probably reflects the surroundings of the villa at the time. The first scene shows two servants dressed in short tunics with two dogs, one tawny and one grey, on leashes. The two animals also appear in the scene on the immediate right, in the act of attacking a fox. In the second episode a huntsman (Constantius Chlorus) offers a sacrifice to Diana the Huntress, placing incense in a brazier on the altar in front of a column on which a statue of the goddess stands. Behind him another huntsman, Constantine, son of Constantius and future Emperor, watches while holding the reins of his black horse. Another young huntsman (probably the son of Maximian because of the ivy-leaf decoration on his tunic, which was the symbol of the Imperial family) appears on the right of the sacrificer, also holding a horse by the reins. The scene is completed on the left by two characters carrying a wild boar, and on the right by a young man with a dog and a huntsman holding the hare he has bagged in his left hand. In the third register two falconers are watching two thrushes perched on a laurel bush; one of them is preparing to release his falcon. The fourth register shows the grey hound attacking a fox as it tries to take refuge in its lair, and the various stages of the capture of a hare, which is first pursued by the two hounds and then run to earth by a mounted huntsman, shown striking it with a lance. The fifth episode shows the exciting capture of a group of deer, chased towards a net by mounted huntsmen. A dramatic moment from a wild boar hunt is shown on the right; the animal tries to attack a fallen huntsman, while above it another huntsman holds a rock in both hands, ready to hurl it at the boar to defend his companion. A magnificent scene in the middle of the mosaic portrays the hunt banquet, held in a clearing surrounded by greenery. Against the background of two cypresses, a red canopy has been stretched between two oak trees, and the circular brazier used to roast the game stands beneath it. Behind the huntsmen sitting down to the banquet (two of which have damaged faces), a black and a bay horse are tied by their reins to two trees. Servants are bustling round the diners; one is offering a jug of red wine, one is taking bread or other food from a wicker basket, another is holding out a goblet and lastly, a negro kneeling on the ground on the left is blowing on the flames to rekindle the fire.

Detail of floor mosaic

THE OCTAGONAL-MOSAIC ROOM

The floor is decorated by a mosaic (interrupted at the top left by a well dating from the Norman period), with a complicated pattern of octagons bordered by a double braid and enclosing medallions decorated with a rose in the middle.

Traces of the original paintings still survive on the walls of this room, which was intended for the servants of the dominus.

Detail of mosaic floor

THE SQUARE-MOSAIC ROOM

This room, preceded by the Octagonal-Mosaic Room which acted as a vestibule, still retains part of the original floor mosaic, with its geometrical pattern featuring squares of two different sizes, edged by a black frame and multicoloured braids, and enclosing rosettes, four-petalled flowers and other floral motifs.

Detail of mosaic floor

THE GREAT HUNT AMBULATORY

This magnificent corridor, some 60 metres long, runs parallel to the eastern side of the peristyle, to which it is connected by a colonnaded gallery with elegant marble plutei connecting columns with capitals of mixed Ionian and Corinthian orders. The rectangular ambulatory, which terminates in two large exedrae on the shorter sides, connected the Imperial family's private apartments at the sides of the great basilica to the basilica itself. The magnificent figured mosaic covering the floor of the corridor portrays various hunting episodes which take place in the furthermost provinces of the Empire, starting with the capture of wild beasts and concluding with their transport to Rome, where they were used for games at the Circus Maximus. The two exedrae of the ambulatory are decorated with portrayals of two women, surrounded by animals, personifying Africa and India (or Asia). Africa is depicted as a girl with dark skin and curly black hair, holding an elephant's tusk in her left hand; next to her, on her left and right, are an elephant with a latticework skin and a phoenix, the mythical bird that rises from its own ashes. The figure of India, wearing a white tunic and flanked by a bear and a panther, features in the mosaic decorating the opposite exedra, many parts of which are missing.

Details of floor mosaic

35

The long rectangle running between the two exedrae is decorated with a mosaic depicting hunting parties and the transport of captured animals. The composition begins with hunting scenes in the five provinces forming the dioceses of Africa (Mauritania, Numidia, Tripolitania, Proconsular Africa and Byzacena), represented by realistic landscapes with wooded hills, watercourses, marshes and plains, which serve as the background for porticoed buildings inhabited by men armed with lances and shields, and animals. In addition to lively scenes of animals hunting their prey (including a panther attacking an antelope and a leopard chasing deer), the

Details of embarkation of animals

mosaic shows an animal captured in each province – panthers, antelopes, wild horses, a Barbary lion and a wild boar. This is followed by a scene showing the transport of the captured animals on ox-drawn carts to a sailing ship anchored in a harbour (presumably Carthage), where they are placed in special cages; slaves are shown loading a billy-goat and two large ostriches. In the middle of the corridor, in front of the entrance to the basilica, some officials are depicted wearing rich tunics and the characteristic Pannonian cap, watching the animals being unloaded in Ostia harbour, from where they would be taken to Rome. The scene continues with another sailing shop,

1) Capture of a rhinoceros
2) Detail

probably anchored in the port of Alexandria, onto which slaves are forcibly loading an elephant and a rhinoceros.

Other hunting episodes show the capture in the Nile delta of dromedaries, tigers, a hippopotamus and a rhinoceros, very realistically depicted with its legs in the water as a result of the use of paler tesserae for the lower part of the body than the upper part. A character watching the hunt flanked by two soldiers bearing shields has been identified as the Emperor Maximian Herculius; in fact, the soldier on his left has a badge on his right shoulder decorated with the ivy leaf, the symbol of the Imperial dynasty. There are more hunting scenes at the

1-2) Details of the capture and transport of animals
3) Maximian protected by two soldiers

38

end of the long corridor, showing the capture of tiger cubs and a gryphon by soldiers, and a lion attacking a donkey.

Among the soldiers engaged in the wild beast hunt, take a close look at the one armed with a shield, near the scene of the lion attacking a deer; he is wearing a short tunic on which a swastika appears. The swastika symbolised the rotation of the sun, personified by the divinity of the four seasons.

1) Soldiers capturing animals
2) Personification of Africa

THE CHECKED-MOSAIC ROOM

The vestibule to the Room of the Ten Bikini-clad Girls is decorated with a geometrical floor mosaic in which squares with white borders containing black triangles and four-petalled flowers enclose multi-coloured key patterns and geometrical and floral motifs. Significant traces of the original paintings survive on the walls.

THE ROOM OF THE TEN BIKINI-CLAD GIRLS

This square room, preceded by a vestibule decorated by an elegant multicoloured mosaic floor with a geometrical pattern framed by a braided strip, is situated at the end of the southern portico of the peristyle. There are traces of the original sectional frescoes on the walls, while the floor has an interesting superimposed mosaic decoration. The first and oldest mosaic, probably contemporary with the other mosaics in the villa, can be identified in the top left-hand corner; it features a series of tessellated squares with braided edges that intersect to form stars, which contain tondi. The second mosaic, which covers almost the entire floor, was laid over the previous one, perhaps around the 4th century A.D.; it portrays 10 girls (though all that remains of one of them is the lower part of the legs) performing gymnastic exercises. Their scanty clothing, consisting of briefs and a strip of material covering the breast, is very similar to the modern bikini. The upper register, from which nearly the whole figure of the first girl is missing, shows (from left to right) one girl jumping while carrying weights, one throwing the discus, and two running. In the lower register (from right to left) two girls are playing ball, one is wearing an entwined wreath and holding the palm of victory in her left hand, and another is holding a spoked wheel in her left hand and is also about to receive the symbolic

The room of the ten bikini-clad girls

prizes for the winner (the entwined wreath and the palm) from the girl with the gilded tunic on the left. The scene has been interpreted in various ways by experts, including a portrayal of gymnastic exercises performed after bathing or special exercises performed in the water by the girls.

Details of the room of the ten bikini-clad girls

THE DIAETA OF ORPHEUS

This large rectangular living room, probably used for listening to music, had an apse in the end wall and was decorated by a square fountain in the middle. A plinth built against the wall at the end of the apse supported a Roman marble copy of Praxiteles' Apollo Lyceius, only the bust and head of which survive. The floor is covered by a magnificent mosaic framed by a border strip decorated with laurel leaves, in which the myth of Orpheus is portrayed. In the middle of the composition Orpheus sits on a rock, clad in a purple cloak and a pair of red sandals, intent on playing the lyre; his absorbed features betray his melancholy, reminding the observer of the sad loss of his beloved wife Eurydice.

Around him, surrounded by the greenery of a tree and a few shrubs, are numerous animals portrayed with incredible realism, down to the smallest detail.

In addition to the larger ones, such as the horse, dromedary, fox, deer, peacock, goose, falcon, tiger, antelope and bear, there are also some small birds, a lizard, a snail, a tortoise, a porcupine, and even mythical animals like the gryphon and the phoenix.

View of the beautiful rectangular room, with the statue of Apollo Lyceius

The mosaic picture is completed by three panels with borders decorated by laurel leaves framing other animal figures.

According to the legend, Orpheus, son of the muse Calliope and Oeagrus, lost Eurydice, who died after being bitten by a snake she had trodden on when fleeing from the shepherd Aristaeus, son of the god Apollo, who intended to marry her. The inconsolable Orpheus descended to Hades, which was guarded by Cerberus, the terrible dog who prevented the living from entering the kingdom of the dead, and sent the dog to sleep with the sweet sound of his lyre. On hearing his wonderful music the rulers of the underworld, Hades and Persephone (the Pluto and Proserpine of Latin mythology), took pity on him, and gave him permission to take Eurydice back with him to the world of the living, provided that he did not look behind him before leaving Hades. Overcome by joy, Orpheus could not resist turning back to look at his bride, who then vanished, returning to the world of the dead forever. The desperate young man began to play his lyre again, convinced that he could win over the gods, but this time they remained unmoved. However, all the animals of the earth were enchanted by his music, and turned to look at him when they heard him play.

1) View of the Diaeta of Orpheus, portraying animals watching Orpheus as he plays his lyre
2) Statue of Apollo Lyceius

1

TRICLINIUM

This magnificent square room, with three large apses along three sides (the fourth, with two columns, is occupied by the entrance) is entered from the end of the xystus, and was used for official banquets. Each apse, separated from the large central section (which measures 12 x 12 metres) by two marble columns at the entrance, had a marbleclad base in the end wall with a large statue, perhaps portraying an imperial or divine figure, standing on it. The triclinia (couches), on which diners reclined during the banquet, were placed alongside the apsidal sections.

The room has one of the most complex, exquisite floor decorations in the entire villa (although some parts are missing), with grandiose scenes inspired by the Herculean cycle, and especially the famous Twelve Labours which Eurystheus set for Hercules. According to legend, the goddess Hera drove Hercules mad in order to take her revenge on her adulterous husband Zeus (who had fathered Hercules, one of his numerous illegitimate children, by Amphitryon's wife Alcmena). In his madness, Hercules killed two of his own children by the King of Thebes' daughter Megara and two of his nephews, the children of his brother Iphicles. In order to do penitence for these terrible crimes, Hercules travelled to the sanctuary of Delphi to purify himself and consult the oracle.

The triclinium, and floor mosaic portraying the Twelve Labours of Hercules

The oracle instructed him to enter the service of Eurystheus, King of Argos, who ordered him to perform the Twelve Labours. Enclosed in a frame with a meander pattern, the scenes are portrayed on a white background with a dizzying succession of characters (though the hero Hercules never appears), each of which represents one of the 12 episodes in the mythical labours, narrated in a continuous, unified sequence. In the first labour the hero killed the terrible lion of Nemea, unconquerable by weapons, with his bare hands; in the second he killed the Lernaean hydra, portrayed with the body of a serpent and the head of a woman (according to the legend the hydra had nine heads, only

Detail of floor and exterior view of triclinium

52

one of which was mortal); in the third and fourth he captured the Erymanthian boar and the Ceryneian hind, with its copper hooves and gilded horns; in the fifth he killed the bronze-winged Stymphalian birds that fed on human flesh; in the sixth he killed the Amazon Queen Hippolyte for her girdle, which he gave to Eurystheus' daughter Admeta; in the seventh he diverted the waters of the River Alphaeus to cleanse the stables of Augeas, but then killed him because he failed to keep the promise that if Hercules succeeded, he would give him a tenth of his herd; in the eighth he captured the Cretan wild bull and bore it alive on his shoulders to Eurystheus; in the ninth he captured the terrible mares of

Interior view of triclinium and unsaddled rider

Diomedes, King of the Bistones in Thrace, which were fed on the flesh of dead enemies; in the tenth he killed the monstrous three-bodied giant Geryon, and captured his cattle after killing the seven-headed dragon and the dog Orthrus which stood guard over the herd; in the eleventh he took the golden apples from the garden of the Hesperides after killing the two-headed snake guarding the tree and convincing Atlas to let him shoulder the burden of the skies for a moment while Atlas picked him some of the apples; in the twelfth and last, Hercules captured the savage three-headed dog Cerberus, guardian of Hades, and freed Theseus from the kingdom of death. In the south-eastern corner of the composition (which is badly damaged here) there is a sea scene, perhaps alluding to the Argonauts' voyage to Colchis in search of the golden fleece, and a man's head dripping with blood, perhaps that of Amicos, King of the Bebrici, who was punished by Hercules.

The mosaic decorations in the three apses are equally exquisite. In the left-hand apse, a connecting strip between the floor of the main room and the floor of the apse portrays the metamorphosis of Daphne on the left and the metamorphosis of Cyparissus on the right. On the floor of the apse is a scene representing the glorification of Hercules, framed by a double braid. Hercules is in the middle, flanked by two male figures in a poor state of preservation identifiable as Zeus (on the right), crowning the hero, and

The glorification of Hercules

Photo on pages 56-57:
view of the "Titanomachia"

Dionysus or Hercules' faithful companion Iolaus (on the left). The central apse, preceded by a strip depicting the myths of Hesione and Endymion, is decorated with the scene from the Titanomachia in which the five giants who rebelled against Zeus try to rid themselves of the arrows poisoned by the blood of the hydra which Hercules had shot at them. The badly damaged connecting strip in the right-hand apse depicts the heads of a camel and a billy-goat, while the splendid apsidal mosaic portrays the metamorphosis of the Maenad Ambrosia. This episode portrays the murder of the Maenad Ambrosia by Lycurgus, King of Thrace. The King, who caught the god Dionysus celebrating an orgy in his kingdom, ruthlessly banished him, killing many of the satyrs and Maenads who took part in the celebrations with him, and imprisoning many others. To demonstrate his hatred for the Dionysiac rites, Lycurgus prohibited their celebration in his kingdom, and actually had all the vines growing there torn up. Overwhelmed by anger, which eventually drove him mad, the King even killed his own son, mistaking him in his folly for a vine shoot. As the axe with which he committed the terrible deed fell, it chopped off Lycurgus' own legs, and he cried out in pain. By order of Zeus, the satyrs and Maenads imprisoned by Lycurgus then freed themselves, and attacked and killed the King. One of the Maenads killed by the King was Ambrosia, whose metamorphosis into a vine is portrayed in the mosaic. The King, shown naked in the middle of the scene with the vine shoots issuing from the Maenad entwined around his legs, is brandishing his two-edged axe as he tries to strike Ambrosia. Behind her can be seen the god Dionysus, Pan and Silenus wearing a crown of vine leaves. Behind Lycurgus are three more Maenads, one of whom is holding his arm to restrain him and threatening him with the point of her thyrsus, while a naked youth sets a panther, sacred to Dionysus, on the King.

1) *The slaying of the five giants*
2) *Lycurgus on the point of killing Ambrosia (detail)*

1

Lycurgus on the point of killing Ambrosia

THE XYSTUS

From the peristyle, a corridor led to this large open elliptical courtyard, with a row of pilasters running round three sides which originally supported a roof. The pilasters, joined by marble-clad masonry plutei, were interrupted on the fourth side to make room for a deep exedra containing three large niches. The floor of the courtyard was decorated with coloured tesserae forming a zig-zag pattern, framed by a border of white stone slabs; a fountain stood in the middle, and another smaller one stood next to a pilaster on the left of the entrance to the triclinium, at the end of the xystus.

The floor of the portico was far more rich and complex. It was entirely covered with a multicoloured mosaic framed by an elegant denticulated strip; some very realistic busts of animals, including deer, gazelles, lions, hyaenas, tigers, wolves, jackals, goats, ducks, geese and horses were surrounded by large acanthus leaf volutes issuing to right and left from the trunk of the great tree portrayed in the centre.

Lizards, small birds, mice and weasels can also be seen among the volutes.

Six small rooms, connected to the portico by their own entrances, are situated on the longer sides of the courtyard, three on either side. The mosaic decorations in the three rooms along the northern side (a cubiculum on either side and a connecting vestibule in the middle) have the grape harvest as their dominant theme.

The xystus

The mosaic features the erotes/cupids already mentioned, portrayed as pretty cherubs intent on their joyful, busy activity of picking grapes, and a figure identifiable as Dionysus (the Bacchus of Roman mythology and the deity who symbolised the vital force present in all nature, in man and in wine, and was traditionally venerated with orgiastic rites that celebrated the irrepressible energy of nature and instinct) or a satyr, an emblematic figure half man and half goat, often portrayed in banqueting, erotic or other hedonistic scenes in Graeco-Roman art.

Vine growing was probably depicted in the first chamber, to the west, as can be deduced from the few remains of the mosaic floor, on which a pergola and the leg of an amorino can be seen.

The other cubiculum has a lively mosaic floor showing scenes of the grape harvest, with amorini picking bunches of ripe grapes and placing then in wicker baskets.

In the middle of the composition, in a tondo bordered by a wavy pattern, is the wreathed bust of an old man, probably the god Dionysus or a satyr. Transport of the grapes on ox-drawn carts and grape treading form the subject of the mosaic decorating the floor of the central vestibule, also featuring the agile winged figures of numerous amorini.

The three rooms on the eastern side (once again a cubiculum on either side and a connecting vestibule in the middle) had mosaic decorations with scenes of amorini fishing; these are only identifiable in the two bedchambers, while the one in the vestibule no longer survives.

The western cubiculum is decorated with the attractive figure of a putto riding a dolphin on the ocean waves.

1) *Acanthus leaf volutes portraying a gazelle*
2) *Detail of the xystus*
3) *Acanthus leaf volutes portraying a deer*

3

THE CORRIDOR CONNECTING THE PERISTYLE AND THE XYSTUS

The small ambulatory runs from the western corner of the southernmost part of the peristyle, connecting the peristyle to the xystus. According to some experts, this route was used by the Emperor's guests (and the Emperor himself on official occasions) to reach the large triclinium from the four-sided portico via the xystus. A small staircase leads from the entrance to the main corridor: there the mosaic floor, which is in such a poor state of repair that the original detail can only be guessed at, portrays complex acanthus volutes alternating with figures of birds, surrounded by a plain black and white border.

KITCHEN

This huge room, built along the south side of the xystus and the corridor connecting the xystus to the four-sided portico, has been identified by archaeologists as the main kitchen used to prepare food on the occasion of receptions and official banquets held in the triclinium.

Connecting corridor

THE GRAPE-TREADING OECUS

The dominant theme of the floor mosaic in the middle room, which acted as a vestibule to the other two, is the transport of grapes and grape treading; the scene shows amorini alongside ox-drawn carts laden with bunches of grapes being taken to a villa for treading.

THE VINE-GROWING OECUS

Few traces of the floor mosaic survive in the first of the three rooms leading off the north side of the xystus; all that remains of the original multicoloured decoration, which must have portrayed vine growing, is a pergola and the leg of a cherub.

THE GRAPE-PICKING OECUS

The floor mosaic in this rectangular room also portrays a throng of amorini, this time busy with the grape harvest; they are depicted picking bunches of grapes and placing them in wicker baskets. In the middle of the mosaic, in a tondo bordered by a wavy pattern, is the wreathed bust of a man, probably the god Dionysus.

1) *Vine-growing Oecus: remains of mosaic floor decoration*
2) *Grape-picking Oecus: detail of floor*

THE MUSICIANS' AND ACTORS' CUBICULUM

This rectangular room with an apsidal alcove, originally preceded by marble columns, was the bedchamber of Maximian's daughter Fausta. The lunette in the apse is decorated by a magnificent floor mosaic which portrays the Florales, the festival in honour of the goddess Flora. The goddess, who according to Roman mythology had the power to make trees and flowers blossom, was greatly venerated in the Roman world, partly because of her supposed ability to make barren women fertile. The scene, surrounded by flowering rose branches, shows two girls sitting on wicker baskets weaving garlands of roses. There are two more baskets full of flowers under the garlands, which hang by a cord from the branches of the tree depicted in the middle. Among the branches of the tree there is an ivy leaf, half black and half green, the recurrent symbol of the Imperial dynasty of Herculia. The mosaic in the chamber connecting the apse to the rest of the room shows two headdresses, gem-studded and decorated with garlands of roses and palm branches, standing on a table with two bags at the sides which perhaps contain coins, as the figures written on them would suggest.

The floor of the chamber in front of the apse is decorated with a scene in three registers which shows musicians and actors competing, and a person holding the palm to be awarded to the winner together with the prizes on the table. The Greek letters in the picture indicate the various musical notes.

Mosaic with girls plaiting rose wreaths

THE SMALL CIRCUS VESTIBULE

This small rectangular room leads off immediately to the right of the semicircular atrium. The floor is decorated with an amusing scene from the games held at the Circus Maximus. Four chariots driven by young charioteers, one drawn by webfooted birds (white geese) and the others by large birds (red flamingos, blue waders and green doves), follow one another round the central spina of the circus, at the centre of which stands the obelisk of Augustus. Each chariot is accompanied by a young man on foot; three of them are holding an amphora, and the fourth holds the palm of victory, awarded to the green chariot.

Beautiful mosaic floor portraying a two-horse chariot race

THE SEMICIRCULAR ATRIUM

This secluded exedral porticoed atrium, situated opposite the Diaeta of Arion, is connected by two doors to the southern section of the Great Hunt corridor, and has a small tetrastyle portico with marble Ionic columns surmounted by capitals, arranged in a semicircle to enclose a nymphaeum. The floor is decorated by a lively mosaic with a marine subject populated by a throng of amorini, some shown naked and others wearing short tunics, busy fishing from boats. Other amorini are playing with ducks among the waves. Various buildings connected by porticoes stand on the shore in the background.

Detail of the atrium and the floor portraying amorini fishing

THE EROS AND PAN VESTIBULE

This rectangular room, which served as the antechamber to the inner cubiculum, stands on the left of the semicircular atrium, to which it is connected by a door, opposite the Small Hunt vestibule. Slight traces of the original frescoes survive on the walls, while the vivid mosaic floor (partly damaged) portrays the battle between the god Pan, half man and half goat, and Eros, god of love and son of Venus and Mars, in an elegant leaf frame. The portrayal of the contest was probably intended to indicate the need for a strenuous battle by the good but ugly person, represented by Pan, to conquer love, personified by Eros. According to Greek mythology Pan, a son of the god Hermes, was so ugly that his mother fled, horrified at the sight of him, immediately after giving birth; his father carried him to Olympus where he was treated no better, being scorned and ridiculed by the gods. Pan symbolised wild, uncontrolled instinct and irrepressible spirits; in the mythological tradition he was always rejected by the women he fell in love with because of his appearance, forming a sharp contrast with Eros, the god of beauty and love. Behind Pan is the satyr who judged the contest (with a white tunic and red cloak, goatee beard and wreathed head), holding the characteristic stick in his left hand, and two Maenads holding thyrsus branches. Behind Eros are members of the imperial family including Maximian's stepdaughter Theodora, and a servant girl wearing the hairstyle typical of the period. The top register portrays a table bearing the prizes for the winner: four gem-studded headdresses and two bags of coins. Other symbolic prizes (a palm branch and a coin) appear between Eros and Pan.

Large floor mosaic portraying Eros and Pan arguing

74

THE HUNTING YOUTHS' CUBICULUM

This room, which was the bedchamber of the Emperor's son Maxentius, is preceded by the Eros and Pan Vestibule, and has a rectangular alcove originally preceded by marble columns. On the walls are a few remains of the original frescoes with figured sections, later covered with marble slabs of which some trace still remains. Although some parts are missing, the multicoloured mosaic decorating the floor, surrounded by a geometrical border and divided into three registers, retains all the original freshness of the floral subject it represents. The upper register shows two young girls in a flower garden picking roses and putting them in the basket they are holding. The middle register portrays two older girls in a garden, one sitting on a wicker basket and plaiting garlands of roses which are hanging from the branches of the tree in the middle, and the other bending to put down a basket full of flowers, and carrying another flower basket in her left hand. The mosaic decorating the chamber in front of the alcove portrays the scenes of young men hunting after which the room is named, against a background of branches laden with fruit and flowers.

Details of three registers of the mosaic scene on the floor

76

THE DIAETA OF ARION

The grandiose living room, preceded by the semicircular atrium, was probably used by the Emperor's wife and family to listen to poetry and music in private (the magnificent Diaeta of Orpheus was used on official occasions). The rectangular room has a deep apse at the end, preceded by two columns. The floor of the main part of the room is decorated with a vivid multicoloured mosaic featuring a mythological sea subject, one of the most magnificent in the entire Imperial villa because of the complexity of its composition and the wealth of characters portrayed. The floor of the apse is covered with a mosaic portraying the head of the sea god Oceanus, depicted with long hair and a beard formed by seaweed and crayfish claws; numerous sea creatures issue from his open mouth, including fish, octopus, shells and crayfish. The rectangular hall features a magnificent portrayal of the myth of Arion, a poet and musician from Lesbos. According to mythological tradition, Arion, son of the god Poseidon (the Neptune of Latin mythology) was attacked by pirates during a voyage and robbed of all his possessions. Just before being killed by the robbers, the poet was allowed to make a last request, and began to play his lyre with such beauty and rapture that the gods took pity on him, and caused his

General view of floor

78

enchanting music to attract numerous dolphins to the pirate ship. Arion, with great presence of mind, jumped overboard and rode a dolphin to safety, reaching Laconia, where he was welcomed by King Periander who immediately punished the pirates. The figure of Arion stands out in the middle of the composition, below a red drape held by two amorini; he is depicted half-naked, riding a large dolphin and playing the lyre he holds in his left hand. Around him are the Nereids (some sitting on rocks or riding sea creatures, others swimming, and all wearing the hairstyle typical of the period) and other mythological inhabitants of the sea including tritons, their hair decorated with crayfish claws, and centaurs holding caskets full of pearls. The sea nymphs (the best-known of whom was Thetis, mother of the hero Achilles) were the daughters of Nereus, the ancient god of the sea. Triton, the ancestor of the tritons, often shown as half man and half fish, was the son of Poseidon and the Nereid Amphitrite. The father of the centaurs, Centaurus, was born of a strange union between Ixion, King of the Lapithae, and a cloud which Zeus caused to resemble his wife Hera, to prevent her from being seduced by Ixion, who had fallen in love with her. Alongside these characters there are a myriad of sea, land and mythological creatures (including dolphins, tigers, lions, leopards, panthers, wolves, deer, sea horses, bulls, gryphons, octopus,

Details of the Diaeta of Arion

80

snakes, crayfish and a variety of fish), some ridden by winged putti, which act as a lively border to the central picture.

Detail of a Naiad

THE OCTAGONAL LATRINE

This elegant latrine outside the villa was reserved for the Imperial family. In addition to the remains of the ancient wall frescoes, the elegant floor mosaic still survives; it portrays a vase containing branches of ivy, the plant that symbolised the Herculius dynasty. The latrine originally had marble seats, now lost.

THE CENTENARY BASILICA

This large rectangular hall, with an apse in the end wall, is built on a raised platform adjacent to the central part of the Great Hunt corridor, to which it is connected via an entrance preceded by a flight of four steps and flanked by two red granite columns that originally supported the marble architrave.

The majestic hall was used for the Emperor's official receptions. Two columns stood at the entrance to the apse at the end of the hall; a deep niche in the middle of the apse contained a marble statue of Hercules, only the head of which survives (and is now housed in the museum). Under the niche was the throne, raised on a platform with a masonry seat. The floor of the apse, made of opus sectile, was decorated with geometrical patterns, and had an elegant marble decoration in front of the throne consisting of a tondo framed by palmettes and acanthus flowers. The large room preceding the apse, which probably had a trussed roof, contains few traces of the original mosaic floor, which must have imitated the patterns used in the apse, with rectangles, squares and tondi. Slight traces of the original marble facing remain on the walls.

Detail of apse floor

THE ULYSSES AND POLYPHEMUS VESTIBULE

This quadrangular room, entered from the Great Hunt corridor, is situated on the left of the Centenary Basilica, and acted as the entrance and connecting chamber between the two adjacent cubicula. The richly decorated mosaic floor portrays a scene inspired by an episode recounted in the 9th book of Homer's Odyssey; the protagonists are the Cyclops Polyphemus and Ulysses, together with some of his travelling companions. In the middle of a dark cavern excavated in the rock of Mt. Etna, whose vegetation-covered flanks can be glimpsed in the background, appears Polyphemus, portrayed with a monstrous third eye in the middle of his forehead in accordance with ancient iconography; he is sitting on a rock with a slaughtered ram on his knees, ready to be eaten.

According to Greek tradition the Cyclopes, the sons of Uranus and Gea, were divided into three groups: the storm Cyclopes, the Hecatoncheires and the volcano Cyclopes, Thracian giants who had concentric circles symbolising the sun tattooed in the middle of their foreheads. The fact that they were believed to live in volcanoes explains why the monstrous third eye (which at some stage became the giants' only eye in illustrations) was believed to symbolise the mouth of a volcano. Homer followed this tradition. In the Odyssey he describes Polyphemus as a shepherd who lived in a cave on Etna, and

General view

almost seemed to be one with the volcano ("…nor did he in the least resemble the race that feeds on bread, but rather the summit of a huge mountain"); in fact the passage about the blinding of the Cyclops, from whose eye a torrent of blood gushed forth, immediately recalls the lava flowing from a volcano. The designer of the mosaic in this room of the villa remained faithful to this interpretation, but followed the ancient tradition by depicting the Cyclops with three eyes instead of the single eye described by Homer. An interesting theory postulates that at the time when the mosaic was created, not one but three huge craters could be seen on Etna, and the artist, in his desire for realism, showed them on the face of the personification of the volcano. On the left of the giant, Homer's hero Ulysses, wearing a short tunic and a cloak with his head covered, approaches the Cyclops to offer him a goblet of red wine. Next to him, two of his companions in misfortune are pouring more wine into a large goblet with the intention of intoxicating the giant. The scene is completed by sheep and goats from Polyphemus' flock grazing all around. In Homer's account, the episode ends with Ulysses and his companions escaping from the cavern clinging to the belly of the sheep after the Cyclops has been blinded.

General view of floor mosaic portraying Ulysses and Polyphemus

CUBICULUM WITH EROTIC SCENE

This room, entered from the Ulysses and Pan vestibule, was the Emperor's bed-chamber, and has a rectangular alcove preceded by two masonry pilasters. Traces of the original frescoes, depicting a Maenad and a satyr in diamond-shaped frames, can be seen on the restored walls. The floor of the alcove is decorated by a mosaic with a geometrical subject framed by a border on a dark background, with circles which partly overlap to create floral patterns. The rectangular section, with two pilasters, is decorated with a scene depicting four children (two boys and two girls) playing with balls. The rest of the floor is covered with an elegant mosaic consisting of a complex pattern of interweaving squares, hexagons and eight-pointed stars with masks and busts of women inside them. A large tondo in the middle of a composition, edged by a laurel wreath and framed by a dodeca-gon, portrays an erotic scene: a half-naked girl seen from behind is embracing a seated youth wearing a wreath and holding a situla in his left hand.

The scene is surrounded by four hexagons containing figures of girls symbolising the seasons, and four large stars formed by eight interweaving squares containing masks symbolising the festival of the Saturnalia.

The seasons are represented here by young women wearing hair-styles typical of the period and colourful clothes whose shades recall the typical characteristics of the season symbolised. The masks portraying the Saturnalia, the festival in honour of the god Saturn traditionally celebrated in the Roman world from 17th to 19th December, are also female. The festival commemorated the myth of the Golden Age, the legendary period in which Saturn, whose throne had been usurped by his son Jupiter, descended to earth and took refuge in Latium. He was kindly received by Janus, who from then on ruled over the region with him, teaching men the techniques of tilling the fields and the rules of civilised life. This legendary reign was later renamed the Golden Age because peace and prosperity were guaranteed to all men, who could live their lives in accordance with the ideals of equality and fraternity. During the Saturnalia, which were based on this legend, normal city business came to a halt, a temporary truce was called in current wars, and social roles were reversed (slaves were freed for a few days, wore masks and dressed as masters), so that at least for the duration of the festival, mankind could savour the delights of the Golden Age again. The modern carnival probably derives from the Saturnalia tradition.

General view with bedroom and detail of floor

Photo on page 92:
Erotic scene from floor mosaic in ante-chamber

90

THE FRUIT CUBICULUM

This was the Emperor's wife's bedchamber. It consists of a rectangular section terminating in an exedra, with slender masonry half-columns at its entrance, which contained the bed recess. The walls were decorated with paintings, most of which have been destroyed.

There is an attractive floor mosaic portraying various kinds of fruit in medallions in the rectangular section of the cubiculum, and fish-scale motifs framing a tulip in the exedra.

Details of floor with octagons

PIAZZA ARMERINA

INTRODUCTION

The town, famous mainly because of its closeness to the magnificent Roman Villa at Casale, contains numerous important monuments and relics of various ages: Roman, Mediaeval, Gothic and Baroque.

Piazza Armerina, situated amid the lush countryside of Enna Province, dates from a period prior to the Roman era, but no trace of the pre-Roman settlement remains. However, the historical events in which it played a leading part in Roman times are well known. During the Roman period the nucleus of what was to become the present town developed around the hunting lodge of the Imperial dynasty; it was inhabited until the Arabs invaded Sicily, and was then abandoned until the advent of the Normans. When the Normans arrived around the year 1000, the town took the name of Platia and increased in importance, especially in the agricultural, commercial and military fields. Some troops of Lombard soldiers settled in the vicinity of the town in 1060; after fighting under Count Roger de Hauteville and liberating Sicily from the Arabs, they decided to stay on the island.

A hundred years later the Lombard troops rebelled against King William the Bad and sought shelter in the town of Platia, where they fought the townspeople and seized the Norman castle. The King's reaction was immediate and devastating. He marched to Platia with his troops and decided to punish the rebels; he forced the population to abandon the town, and then ordered his soldiers to destroy it. Amid these scenes of violence and disorder the Imperial villa was damaged by fire and had to be evacuated. It was permanently abandoned after the building was buried under a landslide from the slopes of Mt. Mangone. Only after he had wreaked his vengeance with the destruction of Platia did William the Bad realise that the unfortunate inhabitants had played no part in the rebellion, and he authorised them to rebuild the town using the very stones he had razed to the ground.

Rebuilding work began two years later, not on the site of the ancient Platia but on the Mira hill, where Piazza Armerina now stands. With the aid of special privileges granted by King William after its destruction, the town recovered and achieved a high level of development, not only in the field of town planning but also in the economic, artistic, cultural and military spheres, which further increased in later centuries. Some examples of this splendour are the magnificent palazzi and churches of the Baroque period, built as a result of the prosperity that Piazza Armerina enjoyed for many long years.

The town played a leading part in the Risorgimento and Garibaldi's campaign for Italian unity. One of its most famous citizens was General Cascino, who commanded the Avellino brigade and was awarded the gold medal for military value in the First World War. General Cascino is commemorated by an imposing monument erected by the town council.

1) The Garibaldi Theatre
2) The Garibaldi Villa

THE NORMAN PAGEANT

Around the year 1060, Sicily was liberated from Saracen oppression by Count Roger, brother of Robert Guiscard and son of Tancrède de Hauteville. Every year, the Norman Pageant held at Piazza Armerina commemorates the magnificent entry of Count Roger's troops into the town.

Photo by R. Marino (pp. 98-99) published by kind permission of the Piazza Armerina Tourist Board.

PIAZZA ARMERINA: THE TOWN

A visit to the town might start at the Garibaldi Gardens, overlooking the long Viale Generale Ciancio.

Nearby stands the ancient Church of Santo Pietro, of Renaissance origin, interesting for its 17th-century marble sarcophagi.

A little further on, on the right-hand side, the monument to General Antonio Cascino recalls the courage and humanity of this hero of Piazza Armerina.

The road on the left (Via del Carmine) leads to the 16th-century Carmine Church, with a cloister of the same period, while the road which continues to the right leads to Piazza Umberto I.

Here, preceded by a staircase, stands the church of Santo Stefano, built in the 16th century, which has an interesting façade with a belltower in the attic storey. Opposite the church are the elegant Garibaldi Theatre and the impressive apse of the Romanesque Church of San Giovanni di Rodi (13th century). Nearby, in Largo San Giovanni, stand the quadrangular Torre Padre Santo, a tower which was once part of the mediaeval walls, and the monastery of San Giovanni Evangelista, with the adjacent church decorated by exquisite frescoes.

View of right-hand side of Cathedral

On the opposite side of the square is the Baroque Church of San Lorenzo, its portal flanked by statues of Sant'Andrea Avellino and San Gaetano Thiene.

Beyond San Lorenzo is the 17th-century Church of San Vincenzo, standing next to the magnificent Dominican monastery which now houses the town's seminary. The complex, which dates from the 15th century, was renovated in the Baroque period; all that remains of the original late Mediaeval building is the magnificent portal in the cloister and two elegant mullioned windows in the chapter-house.

The nearby Piazza Garibaldi contains another important Baroque monument, the church of San Rocco.

This severe building, erected in 1613, has a magnificent portal on the main façade, preceded by a staircase.

The Palazzo di Città on the left of the church, formerly a Benedictine monastery, has some elegant frescoes of the late Baroque period in the lovely first floor drawing room.

From here, Via Vittorio Emanuele II leads to one of the most interesting buildings in Piazza Armerina, the Church of Sant'Anna.

This building, erected during the Baroque period, is unusual for its octagonal plan and its lovely curved façade, preceded by a double staircase.

Interior of the Cathedral

A double staircase also gives access to the church of Sant'Ignazio which stands on the opposite side, next to the former monastery of the Jesuit Fathers.

Next, the road leads to the piazza overlooked by the impressive Aragonese Castle.

The square building, standing on a tall base fortified with ramparts, has stout quadrangular keeps at the corners. It was erected in the late 14th century, when the existing Franciscan monastery on the site was rebuilt in its present fortified form by order of King Martin I of Aragon. From here, Via Floresta leads to Piazza del Duomo, ornamented by the Baroque Palazzo Trigona and dominated by the majestic Cathedral.

The building was erected on the ruins of an older church (of

which the lower part of the bell-tower survives), dating from the 15th century. Construction work began in 1604, and continued for several years.

The tall façade, preceded by a double staircase, gives access to an exquisite interior, with a Latin cross plan and side chapels flanking a nave with no aisles. Numerous works of art, some

1) *Church of Sant'Ignazio*
2) *Jesuit School*
3) *Piazza Generale Cascino*
4) *Four Canals Fountain*

of which belonged to the earlier church, embellish the magnificent Baroque architecture, crowned by a dome over 76 metres tall. In the immediate vicinity of the town are the elegant, austere Priory of Sant'Andrea, with the oldest church in Piazza Armerina.

This church, built in 1096 by order of Roger I's nephew Simon Butera, has elegant portals surmounted by pointed arches on the façade and the sides; the interior, which has a Latin cross plan, was originally decorated with magnificent frescoes, painted at various periods between the 12th and 15th centuries. The nearby monastery of Santa Maria del Gesù has an attractive 15th-century portico with an elegant loggia running along it. Other interesting sights near the town are the ruined castle of Roger the Norman, and the Sanctuary of Maria Santissima at Piazza Vecchia, not far away, the destination of a traditional religious procession every April. Another famous ceremony is the Palio dei Normanni (Norman Pageant), held in August to commemorate the entry of Roger the Norman's army into the town.

1) Palazzo Trigona della Floresta by night
2) Santa Maria del Gesù Convent
3) Priory of Sant'Andrea

1

MORGANTINA

INTRODUCTION

Not far from Piazza Armerina, on a flat site in the Serra Orlando district, stand the ruins of another ancient town which bears witness to the cultural vivacity and splendour of Greek and Roman Sicily: Morgantina. This town, of very ancient traditions, originated with a settlement occupied from the Bronze Age by populations of local origin, the Sicani. The original village (of which nothing remains but the ruins of a group of tombs) later passed into the hands of the Morgeti, a population from the Appennines which landed in Sicily in about the 9th century B.C. and occupied much of the island. The ruins of some huts, found mainly on Monte Cittadella, belong to this second period.

In the 6th century B.C. a group of Chalcidian colonists came to Morgantina from Catania, one of the towns founded by the Greeks on Sicilian soil as from the 8th century B.C.. These newcomers were responsible for extending and reorganising the town situated on Monte Cittadella, which was soon transformed from a small village to a functional fortified town with public and private buildings and sanctuaries. The rapid expansion of Morgantina, partly due to increased olive, grape and corn growing on its territory, did not go unnoticed, and led to frequent episodes of destruction during its history.

The town was destroyed for the first time in the mid-5th century B.C. by order of Hippocrates, the tyrant of Gela. Hippocrates aimed to take control of all the coastal towns founded by the Ionian Greeks, and included among them Morgantina which, though inland, had been founded by a group of colonists from Ionia. The town was destroyed again just over 3 decades later, this time by the indigenous Siculian populations which aimed to re-establish the independence of the islands and its towns inhabited by Greek colonists. Morgantina, which was viewed as the prototype of the Hellenised Siculian towns, did not escape the devastation.

A century later, in the second half of the 4th century B.C., more Greek colonists were summoned to Sicily by Timoleon, who had delivered the island from the Carthaginian threat. They settled in Morgantina, rebuilt the town, increased the number of its buildings and extended the city walls. Further improvements were made to the town until the 3rd century B.C., first under the rule of Agatocles, tyrant of Syracuse, and above all in the time of his successor Hiero II, during whose reign Morgantina reached the height of its glory.

On the death of Hiero II the new tyrant Hieronymus failed to continue the neutral policy of his predecessor; he formed an alliance with the Carthaginians and rebelled against Rome. This attitude led to the destruction not only of Syracuse but also of Morgantina, which had followed the new policy. It later became a decuman town of the Romans, and in 35 B.C. Morgantina was destroyed for the last time, by Octavian, to punish the town for taking Pompey's side against him after the death of Julius Caesar.

MORGANTINA: THE EXCAVATIONS

Excavation work conducted in the Morgantina area in the Fifties brought to light numerous remains of the ancient town, mostly dating from the two periods of Greek colonisation – the first around the 6th century B.C., and the second, between the 2nd and 3rd centuries B.C., by new colonists summoned to Sicily by Timoleon. Even earlier are the ruins of tombs excavated in rock and numerous relics found in them, belonging to the original Sicanian village, and the remains of rectangular and circular huts excavated on Monte Citadella and in the San Francesco region, which date from the Morgetic period of the town. The numerous finds discovered during the excavations are now displayed in the archaeological museum of the nearby town of Aidone.

The monuments which can be seen on the Morgantina site stand in what was once the town centre. Immediately after the entrance stood the main agora (measuring 120 x 140 metres), followed by a second, smaller agora a little further to the south. The large agora, which dates from the rule of the tyrant Agatocles (317-289 B.C.), was the place where the political life of the town was carried on. It was surrounded on three sides by porticoes (stoa).

View

The eastern porticoes, which originally had a colonnade preceded by pilasters supporting the roof, were used for political meetings; there were a number of shops along the western side, which was reserved for business activities, and a gymnasion, the building used for sports activities, was constructed in the northern porticoes. The remains of a fountain with a double basin stand at the corner of the eastern and northern stoa, while the rectangular building that housed the Senate (boule) stood in the opposite corner, between the northern and western porticoes. The bouleuterion, preceded by a courtyard and a tetrastyle portico, had a large assembly hall for the 500 senators, who sat on semicircular tiers of seats, no trace of which remains. The macellum, where food was sold, stood nearer to the south-eastern corner of the agora. This square building (2nd century B.C.) was served by a west-facing entrance; the two small rooms on either side of the entrance probably contained statues of deities. Thirteen shops divided between the northern and southern sides overlooked the large inner courtyard, at the centre of which stood a small building, perhaps used as a fish market.

The Graeco-Roman Theatre

Opposite the south side of the macellum stand the ruins of one of the most important buildings in Morgantina, the ekklesiasterion. Formed by a large staircase with 15 rows of steps, at the foot of which was the orchestra area including the base of a raised dais, it was used for meetings of the city assemblies in which the laws issued by the Senate were discussed. The political life of the town was conducted in the prytaneion, the rectangular building standing in the south-eastern corner of the agora. This building,

Doric columns and general view of circular enclosure of the chthonic sanctuary

Photos on page 115: Morgantina, the excavations

which comprised nine rooms giving onto a colonnaded atrium, was used for meetings of the 50 magistrates, and contained the hearth sacred to the goddess Hestia, tended by the Vestal Virgins. Warehouses used for corn storage gave onto the smaller agora; the remains of two terra-cotta kilns have been found near these granaries.

The large town theatre, built in the 4th century B.C., stands on a hillside to the south-west of the large agora. The complex, which held 5000 spectators, was used for town meetings until the ekkle-siasterion was built in the agora. It has the same structure as the ancient theatres, with the cavea destined for spectators divided into two sectors (ima and summa cavea), the orchestra for the choir with the sacrificial altar consecrated to Dionysus, and the stage opposite.

A sanctuary dedicated to the patron goddesses of the town, Demeter and Kore, has been found opposite the theatre. The sanctuary was divided into two sectors, and included the sacred enclosure with the pit in which the blood of sacrificial victims was collected.

Some private houses of considerable interest have been identified in the residential district to the east of the large agora, such as the elegant Salutation House (or Doric Capital House) and the noble House of Ganymede, so called after a mosaic floor depicting the Abduction of Ganymede.

Photos on pages 116-119: general views and details of theatre

INDEX